Mostly Coast People

UNIVERSITY OF WINNIPEG, 515 Portage Ave., Winnipeg, MB. R3B 2E9 Canada

BOOKS BY HUBERT EVANS

Novels

> *The New Front Line*
> *Mist on the River*
> *O Time In Your Flight*

Poetry

> *Whittlings*
> *Endings*
> *Mostly Coast People*

Junior Novels

> *Derry of Totem Creek*
> *Derry, Airedale of the Frontier*
> *Derry's Partner*
> *Mountain Dog*
> *Son of the Salmon People*

Biography

> *North to the Unknown*

Short Fiction

> *The Silent Call*
> *Forest Friends*

MOSTLY COAST PEOPLE

Selected Verse
by
Hubert Evans

Foreword by Margaret Laurence

Harbour Publishing
1982

MOSTLY COAST PEOPLE
COPYRIGHT © CANADA 1982 HUBERT EVANS

ISBN 0-920080-41-3

HARBOUR PUBLISHING
BOX 219 MADEIRA PARK
B.C. V0N 2H0

COVER PAINTING BY JOAN WARN

PUBLISHED WITH ASSISTANCE FROM THE CANADA COUNCIL

PRINTED AND BOUND IN CANADA

Contents

Contents Continued:

FOREWORD

I have never met Hubert Evans, but I feel privileged to call him my friend, for I have met him through his books and through letters. *Mist on the River*, his splendid novel about the native peoples in northern B.C., was first published in 1954, but I did not read it until later, in the New Canadian Library edition, which fortunately brought the book back into print and assured its continued availability. This novel moved me a great deal and taught me a great deal, not by any didacticism but by the simple power of the writing and the ways in which the reader is given the sense of truly living characters caught up in the conflict between the old ways of the villages and the new and oppressive ways of the fish canneries. This is a tragic novel, but it also proclaims the strength of the human spirit.

Enthusiastically, I mentioned *Mist on the River* to Silver Donald Cameron, writer, colleague and friend, and asked him if he had read it. Not only had he read it, but he was actually planning soon to go to B.C. and interview Hubert Evans. He suggested that I write and tell Evans how much I admired the novel. Rather hesitantly, I did so, not knowing what the response might be. I need not have worried. Very soon I got a cordial letter back. Hubert was then in his late 80's and was being forced by failing eyesight to learn touch-typing. He apologized for the errors. It was then that I began to realize the marvellous nature of the man. Learning touch-typing, under such conditions, was no big deal for him. As a very long-time writer, fisherman, union volunteer, a builder of his own house at Roberts Creek, partner in a long and loving marriage, a father, grandfather and great-grandfather, learning to touch-type, with minimal eyesight and at that age, was just something to be dealt with in a commonsense way, with the wisdom and sheer determination acquired over many years.

I subsequently came to know that Hubert Evans had published his first book in 1926, the year I was born. Throughout his writing life, a large number of stories, serials, and children's books have appeared. For years he earned his living partly as a writer and partly as a fisherman. *Mist on the River* must now be regarded as a Canadian classic. The publication of his novel, *O Time in your Flight*, in 1979, was a very special event. This fine autobiographical novel tells of one year in a boy's life, that year being 1899, when the century turned. The picture of life in those times is done vividly and in fascinating detail. The book is a true gift, not only to my generation but to my children's generation and all generations to come.

I recall Silver Donald Cameron saying once, when he was about 40, that when he grew up he would like to be Hubert Evans. Well, at 56 I have some of the same feelings. Hubert is now 90, and has kept the faith all these years. In this terrifying world, we must try, as writers, to proclaim life and its worth, for as long as it is given to us to do so. Hubert Evans has done this and he continues to do so.

The poems in this present collection speak directly to me, and to the deepest parts of my belief. Frequently, they contain a compassionate humour, and this kind of humour is a gift of grace. They are wise and they are caring, caring in the widest sense about human beings and all creatures dwelling on our earth and the earth itself. He is no tourist in this life. He is a person who undertakes responsibilities and who gives and can receive that basic love which is at the heart of faith. His view of life is essentially, I feel, a religious one, by which I mean a sense of sharing in the holy spirit, of celebrating life and trying to honour and protect it.

Hubert, being himself, would probably laugh at my statement that I believe him to be truly great human being, and a fine writer who has given so much to so many of us. He signs his letters "The Old Journeyman". He is, indeed, that. I like, respect and agree with someone who regards writing not in any pretentious way as his "art" but rather as one's craft, one's trade—which also encompasses the sense of vocation. I think of the words of St. Paul, and although Hubert Evans would never use them in reference to himself, they do apply. "I have fought a good fight; I have finished my course; I have kept the faith."

Many of these poems stay in my mind, but I think of one especially, now:

> "Many times in life I too have forgotten
> whence I came and have beaten my wings
> against barriers which would not yield.
> Whose the hand which guided me to the light?"

Old Journeyman, thanks. We go on learning. We go on journeying.

—Margaret Laurence
Lakefield, Ontario
1982.

AUTHOR'S PREFACE

I think of myself as a storyteller. "Writer" is too general a word for my sort. Storytelling is said to be one of the oldest of the professions – not the very oldest, though in certain instances these two professions tend to overlap.

Several months ago I received a letter from a young man in Vancouver (I judged him to be in his late teens) who said he intended to become a writer and asked if he could come and get my advice on how to go about this. I replied that before he came, he should phone me (collect) and tell me *why* he wanted to be a writer. I told him the reason was important. He did not phone and I have not heard from him since. I wish I could have told him that if, deep down, he was set and determined to be a writer, he would become one, come hell or high water, let the rejection slips fall where they may. Also I would have told him that if being a freelance writer was his notion of how to make an easy living, he had another think coming. If I had spent the same number of hours, days, weeks, months, years blowing whistles in some logging show or pushing grocery buggies in some supermarket, my earnings would have exceeded those I earned by writing. I could have told him that except for a few, a very few, Canadian writers of novels, short stories and poetry receive so little for their work that their incomes fall below the so-called poverty level. And that the few who make it big are as rare as the winners of sweepstakes.

There is another matter I would have taken up with that young man. It concerns writers who set themselves apart from other folk as "creative", the implication being they alone are endowed with creativeness. What presumption! The truth is that our food, our clothing, our houses, the utensils we use, the countless amenities which we take for granted are the creative work of fellow humans who have preceded us or who are our contemporaries everywhere on this old earth. Newton spoke for all of us when he said, "If I have seen farther than other men, it is because I have stood on the shoulders of giants." Einstein elaborated on the statement when he wrote of his indebtedness to "the countless generations of unnamed people". He thought of himself as standing at the top of a pyramid built by others who had gone before. I reflect on these statements and am humbled.

There is yet another pointer I could have given that eager young writer-to-be. Back in the 1920's when I began writing "for the market", I made the mistake of dreaming up characters, complications, action, settings and so on, instead of using what I was familiar with. My fantasizing brought me many rejection slips.

Oh those rejection slips! I think of dear old Charles Lamb, though in his case the rejection came by word of mouth, not printed words on slips of paper. "I have spent my life going up and down other men's stairs" he wrote. Picture him trudging down one side of Grubb Street and up the other, his sheaf of unwanted manuscript (quill-penned manuscript) under his arm knocking on editors' doors—"Not today, Mr. Lamb..." "Your work has merit, Mr. Lamb, but..." "Unfortunately, due to changes in our editorial policy..." The wording may have differed from that of rejection slips nowadays, but the message was the same.

P.W. Luce, an inveterate free-lancer and friend of mine since 1913, seldom allowed rejection slips to get the better of him. "I welcome rejection slips" he was heard to say. "I am papering my bathroom with them." He wrote his own obituary, kept it on file and it was published by the Vancouver Sun the day after his death. No rejection slip for the indomitable Phil for that story. A free-lancer to the very last.

I had my first byline on May 32, 1914. Now, 68 years later, on days when impaired eyesight and the various ills old flesh is heir to—plus Dr. Lubin's admonitions—do not prevent, I sit me down in front of my typewriter and three tape recorders and square away to work on the 17th chapter of a novel I began to write well-nigh two years ago. It is slow work but I intend to keep at it even though it may never see print. As a harried young mother was heard to say about our public school system, "at least it keeps 'em off the streets."

These verses are dedicated to the settlers, commercial salmon fishermen, beach-combers, a boat builder, loggers and day labourers with whom I worked and from whom I learned during my three score years in British Columbia.

Coast People

So here we are, the lot of us –
pilgrims and profligates
builders and upsetters of apple carts
dispossessed and dispossessors.
Which found the life they hoped to find?
Which have shadows in their sunshine still?

Smoke Signals

Cast-iron kitchen ranges, ponderous front room heaters,
have been discarded and rust to nothingness.
Modern fuels have superseded firewood.
Chimneys along this stretch of shore no longer signal.

Time was when a woman coming from feeding her hens
or hanging out her wash, would tell her husband:
"The old gentleman still hasn't lighted his fire.
Let's hope he hasn't had another fall. You'd better go over."

Or:
"I see the new family have their fireplace going,
she must be expecting visitors on the steamer."

And he to her:
"Looks like Jacob went digging clams last night.
He just now touched off his breakfast fire."

In those days Scottie, a man of fixed habits,
provided the settlement's time signal. Fair weather
or foul his smoke appeared at the stroke of six.

Those days, a couple could not sleep late of a Sunday
and have their indolence go unnoticed.

Chimneys have become tight-lipped of late,
our houses do not speak to one another.
Is the time approaching when their occupants also
will have nothing to communicate?

The Whittler

On fine summer afternoons
an old man comes to this beach.
Some days he just sits.
Other days he whittles.

Mostly he whittles shavings.
But when the mood is on him
he whittles toy boats.

His boats are not well shaped.
He knows this and leaves them
for the tide to take.

Heritage

Fifty years ago he cleared this ground.
He respected it and tended it well.
It fed his children.
The bones of their children are strong.

Pioneer O Pioneer

This clearing bought by the labour of his years
is being repossessed.
Invading alders subjugate his little orchard,
fir and hemlock second-growth have overrun
his split rail fences.
Their seed is numberless and ever present.
His seed, who could have held what he had won
is rooted elsewhere.
His strength is spent. He is encircled.
The walls of green are closing in.

Sortings

When he was a little boy in bed with measles
his mother gave him the contents of her button bag to sort.
She said this should keep him occupied for a while.
But so much deciding soon tired him.
So he put all the buttons back into the bag
and just lay down and went to sleep.

Old now, he tries to sort the contents of his years;
loves from passions,
regrets from rejoicings,
the symbols from the symbolized,
Samaritan from Pharisee,
self from selfless,   .
chances taken from chances spurned,
all that has made him as he is.

What a mix-up! Forget it, he tells himself.
But this is not the same as sorting buttons;
he can't get the remembering back into the bag.
And sleep is hard to come by now.

The Prude

Were I to tell him in consoling quotes
"they also serve who only stand and wait"
he would glare, clear his throat and say
"don't give me that."
His bed is directly across the ward from mine
the first on your left as you come in.
I would not call him cantankerous, though at times
he does make trouble for the staff,
particularly the orderlies. Yet it is not they
who deny him bathroom privileges. In spite of them
when he has to go, he goes. He declares
there will be two moons in the sky and one in the ditch
before he will lie abed and piss into a bottle.
The morning he was admitted and while a resident
was examining him, I overheard him ask –
and with understandable concern – if the rough life he led
had brought on this trouble with his waterworks.
The doctor said not and that none other than
His Holiness the Pope had suffered from a similar
affliction. The old man said, "I be goddamned"
and chuckled so gleefully that he started coughing.

A day or so before his operation the head nurse
caught him trying to remove his catheter. She warned him
if he tried that again they would tie his hands.
He said that would be the day.

There is one shapely dark-eyed nurse
who has him eating out of her hand. He calls her Dolly
though I know for a fact this is not her name.
When he needs attention she is the one he wants.
I somehow get the feeling that in his prime
when he hit town after months in some logging camp
there was a certain Dolly who was very special to him.

Don't get me wrong. He is not one of your "dirty old men."
Not him! Evenings after visiting hours
when a nurse comes to give back rubs
he waves her off and refuses to roll over.
I take it he considers a hospital is no fit place
for any such carryings-on.

There Comes a Time . . .

This old cat I befriended
has somehow got it into her head
that I need looking after.
When I start for the garden
she takes the lead,
tail up, pausing frequently
to make sure I follow closely
and don't get lost.
There, she sits on the bench
and oversees my work.
I move between the rows
on hands and knees—
a posture which I suspect
she deems appropriate to my station
in the scheme of things.
Even when I go to the bathroom
she tries to supervise.
Expelled, she mews:
"Are you all right in there?"
I know every nook and cranny
of this old house—
I should, I built it.
But will she permit me to
go from room to room
unaccompanied? Not her!
She makes my every move
a personally conducted tour.

Old cats are perceptive, granted,
and maybe I do, at eighty-two
"need help"
But drat her! does she have to be
so obvious about it?

Back-Slider

My no-nonsense neighbor, an avowed atheist,
scoffs at belief in survival after death.
When his old dog died he made a point of
burying it in a grave overlooking the sea.
"Little Mick loved the water," he explained.

The Advocate

A woman whose place along this shore is
west of mine, reports that kelp stalks
make a tasty pickle.
But her neighbors report that
she still grows cucumbers.

Dogmatist

He tells you what to believe
that the proof's right there in the book.
But when you ask to see the page
he doesn't know where to look.

Quality Control

The Old-timer insists, and rightly,
that shakes should not be laid like shingles
but double, courses overlapping, eave to ridge.
He says be god-damned if he knows what
the world is coming to.

Consensus

She tells him what the forecast is,
he tells her what he reads in the sky.
Together they know what the fishing will be
and whether tomorrow her washing will dry.

Swimmers

There was fire in the sea that moonless summer night.
Trailing scarves of spangled phosphorescence
revealed the rhythmic motion of her limbs.
Her voice held wonder
and a warm and wild delight.

There was fire the long-remembered summer night
we swam together.

Exceptions

Why does she tend those pampered flowers
with such solicitude
when in all else her heart is with
life's wayward ones?

Counter-Attraction

"Oh look!" she cried and pointed skyward.
"The osprey is back!"

It was her face I looked at first,
so great was her delight.

Unrequited Love

"I love the sea," she tells me.
Well and good, dear lady,
but let me caution you
the sea will not reciprocate.
During my years here
within sight of this house
the following have drowned:
1 settler
4 towboat men
3 heedless boys
3 youthful canoeists
3 fishermen
1 toddler
1 bride-to-have-been

As indicated by the foregoing
the sea is not selective.
It does not play favorites.
Unlike Jehovah it has no chosen people.

For Services Rendered

Our wharf shed needs repainting
but the government does nothing.
Not so the gulls.
Regularly, without fail
they line the ridge, squat
and lo! the whitewash is renewed.
They should send their bill to Ottawa.

More on Gulls

When I toss food scraps to my resident gull
it calls its comrades before it eats.
My gull is a Socialist.

When they come, it snatches, squabbles
and competes with the best of them.
My gull is a Capitalist.

My gull is a mixed-up voter at election time.

Departure 1938

The Vancouver-bound steamer is at our wharf.
Members of the immediate family go up the gangplank.
We others stand back a little.
Our settlement has nothing to ship this trip—
Nothing that is except the box there on the wharf shed floor.
The box is of clear, edge-grain cedar and
has spliced rope handles, two on each side.
It was made yesterday by Jock the ship's carpenter
who keeps a supply of seasoned lumber on hand
for occasions such as this.

The winches at the foot of the mainmast chatter
as the cargo board is hoisted and lowered to the wharf.
Four of us, hatless, carry the box and
place it lengthwise on the board.
Two deck hands spread a Union Jack over it.
One, presumably a family man, makes a point of
tucking the covering snugly around his end.
He then steps back one pace and removes his battered cap.
His hatless mate waggles a thumb and finger for the
winchman to hoist away.
The winches' chatter is subdued.
Slowly, slowly the winch drums turn.
The skipper appears on the wing of the bridge,
his visored cap held against his chest
—a sea-going padre pronouncing benediction.
Swinging slightly, the load is raised still higher
and held a moment, outlined against the soft grey sky.
An untucked corner of the covering flutters as the
box descends into the dark hold.

Mooring lines are cast off, the gangplank hauled aboard.
As the ship gets underway
we see its ensign lowered to half-staff.
A man behind me clears his throat with needless vigor,
another rolls a cigarette.
Old Scottie says "aye weel weel"... to no one in particular.
Singly and in pairs we leave.
There are cows or goats to milk,
kindling to be split for morning.
Midway along the wharf I look back.
The ship is on course beyond the reef.
I hear white gulls crying.

At the last our neighbour did not have
too rough a crossing.
He was a plain-spoken man and direct in his dealings.
His departure was in keeping.

Steveston 1926
for Buck Suzuki

MR. MINAMI'S HOUSE stands on piles. When the tide is low he goes down the wharf ladder to his fishing boat. When the tide is high, or when the Fraser is in flood, he can step into his boat from his veranda. The outside of the Minami house is not much to look at but its inside is pleasing. It has grass floor mats, some low bamboo stools, a shiny black stove, a table and a dwarf evergreen in a tub beside its door. The room is very, very clean.

When Mr. Minami laughs, his eyelids flutter like the wings of tiny birds. Mrs. Minami only smiles, bows slightly and clasps her hands, one above the other. The Minami children play on the narrow wharf. When I asked Mr. Minami if he was not afraid one of them would fall into the water he shook his head and laughed. When I said one might, he shook his head again and laughed again.

One afternoon when I came to visit, Mr. Minami was shaping small, oblong pieces of wood. He sawed with a saw which sawed backward and planed with a plane which planed backward. After finishing the pieces he painted Japanese writing on them with a brush which had a bamboo handle. "My cousin going Japan. These for his baggage, say where."

"Your cousin goes on a visit?"

"No. Go home. Sick here." Mr. Minami tapped his robust chest.

"Too bad."

"Yes. Too bad. Oh well..."

When Mrs. Minami is mending nets her fingers move quickly and sometimes as she works she sings, not a song, not a tune, just small high notes, circling around and around not going anywhere. Her children sing only school songs. Her eldest daughter goes to high school and is learning to be a stenographer. She makes marks on smooth paper with a graceful pen.

When the salmon are running strongly, Mr. Minami is very happy. When there are not so many salmon he is not unhappy. But when a snag fouls his net, or when a steamer ignores his riding lights and ploughs through his net he is very unhappy. One evening before Mr. Minami went fishing, he took me into the cabin of his boat. He showed me his Easthope engine and his galley stove with cedar kindling and fir bark laid ready. A narrow roll of paper with Japanese writing in gold and black hung from the ceiling above the steering wheel. When I asked, he said the writing was of Japanese prayers. "Camasami, like this." He bowed his head and rubbed the flats of his hands together. "Every day camasami, good. This boat not sink, Other men only some days camasami not so good. Big wind come. Those men, Oh Camasami, camasami. Too late. Those boats go down sure. Every day camasami good, only some days camasami, no good." He paused, eyes partly closed, head tilted, considering. "I think this country no camasami. Yes?"

"No. But plenty good men, plenty church men."

"Hah, not so good." He shrugged. "Oh well . . ." He was leaving churchmen to their fate. Fate would deal with them. He must go fishing.

Spring Tonic

Christmas is over, long weeks of winter lie ahead.
Then in January the seed man's summer catalogue arrives —
luscious lettuce, tomatoes, corn in living colour,
persuasive paragraphs of succulent superlatives.
My spirit soars, digestive juices flow,
Blessings on this little book and on its sender!
Thanks to them what need have I
of sulphur and molasses?

"As it was in the Beginning . . ."

Roto-tillers help
but gardeners must stoop to conquer.

Immortality

Year after year my neighbour
saved the seeds from his
very best tomato plant
and planted them the following season.
In this way he evolved
a superior strain of the plant.
He gave me the seeds
from last season's generation.

My childless neighbour
died during the winter.
But in my garden
his seed lives on.

Preparation

No one comes to my door.
My phone does not ring.
The surf on my beach is stilled.
The garrulous gulls are not speaking to one another and
the crows are holding their convention elsewhere.
Time hangs heavy in the cedars.
Silence is upon me.
Like white stilettos of frost
it penetrates and probes.
I am uneasy.
The child afraid of the dark hides under the covers.
The infantryman under bombardment sprawls in his slit-trench
and pulls his groundsheet over his head.
Exposed, I seek refuge in radio and shield myself
with inconsequential sound:
open-ended talk shows; off-the-cuff opinions of opinionated
commentators; disc jockeys engaging themselves in time-
consuming conversation; come-on commercials; stock market
quotations highlighted by the nimble calculations of
Messrs. Dow and Jones; the astounding information that the
downtown temperature outside this station has, in the last
half hour, risen, or is it fallen, a full degree and that
the prime lending rate is tending in the opposite direction;
sports reporters reporting unsportsmanlike behavior;
along with the news that some unknown mother's
hitherto unknown son has performed the hat trick
to the delight of nine thousand five hundred and
seventy-four spectators in Atlanta, Georgia.

The child knows daylight will come;
the soldier that the bombardment will cease –
or that he will;
Hearing yet not hearing, I seek cover beneath
this crazy-quilt of trivia.
Why?
Is it because these few hours of silence foretell
the terminal silence which will enfold me at the close?

Release

One window is open. A bee bumbles in.
It circles the room wall to wall
now high, now low, erratically
and with increasing speed.
It has lost direction. Frantically
it beats its wings against a window
which is closed.
I guide it through the open window
and see it soar to sunlight.

Many times in life I too have forgotten
whence I came and have beaten my wings
against barriers which would not yield.
Whose the hand which guided me to the light?

Retreat

Winter rains have set in,
the season of earth's thrifty rotting-down is at hand.
I put away my garden tools.
House-bound I am brought face to face
with that Other Person —
my reluctantly reflective self.

Stormy Weather

Good Friday. Southeast squalls.
Rain. Tender, aspiring grass blades
lose their raindrop pearls
and are brought low
with each succeeding gust
but during the lulls they rise again.

Here in my room I listen
to a highschool choir's recording
of Schubert's Mass Number Two.
Inwardly I join the young singers
in the Kyrie
petitioning not for myself
but for them, that when
in their time they are brought low
by winds of advertisity,
they too
will lift their heads again.

Non-Conformist

The wind is compelling
yet not all the branches sway in unison.

Royal Prerogative

Ting, the high-caste Siamese
struck down and ate
our spring's first hummingbird.

The Show-Off

A gawky young crow tries to balance
on a swaying hemlock tip.
The crow teeters.
It spreads one wing, then the other,
then both.
The swaying ceases.
The crow folds its wings and caws
"Look ma—no hands!"

Galahad

Old plum tree's topmost branch
white with blossom—
knight errant's plume waving challenge
to battlements of sullen cloud.

Confetti

Cherry blossom petals
wind-blown on the grass.
The wedding is over.

Tableau

After a night of frost
a windless morning.
Lady birch trees in the sun
languidly disrobing.

His Belated Thanks to:

Alex the Norwegian rover
for teaching him to make dipnets and also
to sing the clap-hands Christmas song while
dancing around the tree with his wife and children;
Jim, R.N. midshipman, turned trapper
for how to make good bread, fly cast,
pole a Tsimpsean river canoe, and fashion
a bowline, sheet bend and rolling hitch;
Joe, the methodical Dutchman
for how to endure dust-filled hours
in a whipsaw pit;
Harry, the versatile Welsh sailor
for how to plank a dory-skiff
without benefit of steam box;
a Coast Salish matron and
a Hailsa grandmother
for how to split and dry-smoke salmon;
Tom from up-state New York
for how to stay warm in a tent at seventy-two below;
Big John, the hand trolling Finn
for how to make a sure-fire tandem salmon spinner
from twenty-gauge brass;
Yorkshire Fred, for how to build cobblestone fireplaces;
Oscar a bullbucker from God-knows-where
for the proper procedure in filing crosscuts;
the white Russian woman doctor
for how to make borsch
and the lusty Ukranian
for how to relish it;

the Greek scholar
for how to milk goats;
a Cornish man, a Devon man,
a Kentish man, a man of France,
a Geordie, two men from Sussex
for tips on successful vegetable gardening
as well as to Lance, a Texan
who in wayward youth
cooked for Billy the Kid and rode the Chisholm Trail,
for demonstrating the possibility, under ideal conditions,
of maturing sweet potatoes and peanuts
on this southern B.C. Coast.
To these and others from other lands,
again, his belated thanks.

And what, you may ask, had he to teach them?
Very little, I suspect, except that
a sixth-generation Canadian though set in his ways
was not beyond instruction.

Altered Perspective

My young grandson's here and he's brought along
a duck he's had almost since the day it hatched.
He calls it Joe. It's in full adult plumage now
as handsome a mallard drake as ever I set eyes on.
It follows him about the place, the pair of them
gabbling back and forth in some language of their own.
They swim follow-the-leader style
first one duck-diving then the other.
I declare I would never have believed it!

In my day I was a crack wing shot and prided myself
on bagging my limit season after season.
Many a one like Joe I've blasted out of the sky
simply for the sport of it. But right now that's a thing
I'd just as soon forget about..

Al

He talked tough and he was tough.
Trapper, fisherman, hunter
he'd done more than his share of slaughter.
But when kittens had to be drowned
he always warmed the water.

To a Field Mouse This Day Departed
(on entering my eighty-sixth year)

Though I deny full responsibility
for your untimely, not to say unseemly, demise
I freely admit my lack of foresight was
to some degree the cause of it.
Last evening when I discovered you beneath the tub
and shut you in the bathroom overnight I intended
first thing this morning to return you unharmed
to the brush pile whence you came
there to live out your allotted span nibbling
and scampering to your heart's content. Instead
I find you lying face submerged, your tiny hands outstretched
as if in supplication, floating on the water
of my toilet bowl.
If only I had thought to close the lid!
But to my credit be it said I did not flush you down the drain
to dissolution but go now to give you decent burial
among budding briar and yellow broom between
the brush pile and the berry patch.

Granted I share a tendency found among the very old
of waxing watery-eyed and sentimental over might-have-beens
but this morning I so vividly remember times
when through necessity, fear or folly I too
teetered on the ultimate brink
yet was somehow kept from falling.

To a Packrat

It must be said of this particular packrat that he was thrifty
and that to the best of his knowledge he planned ahead.
His deposit box was a shelf in what was formerly
our woodshed. Often he could be heard there,
sometimes at all hours of the night, checking and
rechecking his holdings. These included
a comprehensive selection of bottle caps, common and preferred
plus a large stock of broken china featured by
no less than five teacup handles, three of them gilt-edged.
True, his porcelain doorknob would be hard to move
and he had over-extended himself in clam shells.
However these liabilities were more than compensated for
by a silver teaspoon left on the beach by picnickers, and
six sardine-tin keys, complete with twisted lids.
In addition he held a much sought-after neck of
a blue glass medicine bottle. Bye and large and
things being equal, his future seemed assured
and his declining years amply provided for.

Unfortunately in this world things are seldom equal.
Under the weight of last month's snow, the shed collapsed.
His life's savings were a total loss
and what the future holds for him is anybody's guess.

Risk Capital

In my dream the man is saying:
This geologist fellow tells me and my associates
that ten thousand or so years ago
these choice seafront properties of ours
were under a mile-deep glacier
and eight hundred feet of water
and that, come the next ice age
they may be so again.
I'd thank him to keep his predictions to himself.
They'll depress land values
and discourage long-term investment.

Fog

Today after finishing my Saturday chores
I went hand trolling for late fall cohoes
and was a mile or so off shore when fog rolled in.
Tide running every-which way, water too deep to sound
I completely lost my bearings and would probably
have drifted the Gulf all night in an open boat
except that I chanced to hear what I took to be
our old rooster crowing. Lucky for me it was.
I turned the boat, followed the sound to shore
and landed home in time for supper.

This forenoon if I could have laid hands on him
that rooster'd be in the pot right now
simmering for our Sunday dinner.

Strange sometimes how things work out.

Roundup

Riding Greyhound west from Kamloops
in early morning dawn I see
white-faced cattle in their hundreds
belly-deep in silvered ground mist.
Some will go to summer range again
but for you others
you prime steers and medium heifers
you stockers and feeders
you canners and cutters
you good slaughter cows
and however else they grade you,
stockyard, abattoir, packinghouse await
until as
tenderloin, t-bone, sirloin,
prime rib, rump, round, rolled,
bladed, chuck, minced, flank and brisket
as calves liver from slaughter cows
your various parts and organs
meticulously weighed and priced
you go from meat counters
to strengthen nourish and sustain
workers and the never-idle rich
teachers pupils drop-outs
matriarchs matrons and foetuses
harlots confessing to holy men and vice versa
makers of wars and defiers of laws
bearers of burdens and bearers of sorrows
drivers of buses, poets riding on buses
and
"Cache Creek next and a breakfast stop"

Sunrise outlines your nurturing hills.
I will remember you
all you white-faced sacrificial ones,
I will remember you, uncomprehending and content
standing in silvered mist,
standing in your valley of the shadow.
I will remember.

City Dump

Here in this midden-in-the-making circa 1977
affluent societies' discards lie in open graves.
Here catacomb rats and wintering crows
feast on wasted food enough to plump the cheeks
and still the cries of famished children
in that other world.
Here is once-used paper in abundance
which if reclaimed could record
the wisdom, vanities and follies
our our restless generation.
Here are artifacts cunningly contrived for obsolescence
and status symbols which have ceased to symbolise.
("Trade up to . . ." "You owe it to yourself to . . ."
so went the sales pitch.)
High on a fire-killed fir, black against the sky
a sombre raven sits in judgement.
How long until the account is rendered
payment on demand
for all this squandered wealth of mine and mill
of farm and forest,
for a life span of man-hours brought to nothingness?

How long? The answer comes:
Not long.

Conditioned Reflex

They came here to relax, unwind,
lie on the beach
get the city out of their systems
and as the husband put it
let their souls catch up with their bodies.

Too late they came.
They could not alter the pattern
of their parking meter lives.

Flower Children

They came starry-eyed from the city
to walk with Nature.
But only to her chosen
would she give her hand.

Progress

When he was a boy
he worked with his father in the woods.

When he had a boy
they walked in the woods of a Sunday.

Now that boy has a boy.
But the woods are gone.

"Give us this Day . . ."

At the camping place
I watch a woman burning bread.
As she drops slices onto the open fire
she explains the loaf is not fresh enough
to suit her family.
The slices curl and blacken.
Bread – this bread – the hard-won staff of life!
I shrug and by my silence
condone the sacrilege.

The Big Bright Room

Tiny feathers stuck with blood
to a window of this big, bright room.
And on the ground below, lifeless,
neck awry, bill shattered,
sodden with eave-drip,
the visionary bird.

That bird might be alive today
and singing at my window,
had it but known what old men learn —
and often to their sorrow —
the Big Bright Room, desired today,
will be a cage tomorrow.

Exodus

Those commissars of Ambition, Duty, Need
that in his prime decreed he spend his days
in simulated sunlight within the confines of your concrete caves
have lost their hold on him. Here in this shake shack
in this inlet so like the North Sea fiord of his beginnings
he makes his final stand. Never again will he inhale
the stale exhalations of your traffic, obey your time clocks,
march to the beat of your mass production drums.
Here among these logged-off slopes, thrusting green
testifies to Earth's renewal. But the over-burden
of your vaunted progress denies renewal. You have infected,
fouled her, denied her issue. Your sewers
are worm holes in her vitals.
Vancouver you have seen the last of him.
And when the ending overtakes him here
he will lie in his balsam-feathered bunk,
draw the threadbare blanket over him
and go, content.

A Cry

He is stuck here, as the saying is,
"like a beetle on a pin."
The beetle has wings it can no longer use.
He was never given wings.

Big Olaf

During all the years the mission boat visited the inlet
and held services aboard, he never once attended.
He let it be known, and in no uncertain terms
he had no time for sermons
and little for those who preached them.

The hand-logger who found him dead beside his chopping block
reported the body was on its knees, its huge hands clasped,
its head bowed, for all the world as if in prayer.
Some doubted this. Though in all fairness it must be said
the hand-logger was by no means an outwardly religious man.

Destiny

Salmon ascend clear streams to die,
bottom fish die in the murk.

Extended Care

Their sedated four-dimensional dreams
are of childhoods lived half a world apart.
Here in the crowded ward their beds so near
that if they roused and reached
their hands would meet —
the work-worn brown one
and the wasted, blue-veined white.

Still Life

On this coast
in this season of straight-down rain
cedars in winding sheets of tattered mist.
Hunched raven on a bough, black on black.
Amid enveloping salal, weathered wooden dove
on rusted wire legs
marks the fallen grave house
of some long-forgotten chief.

Ratings

TV aerials among weathered totem poles.
The poles too have matters of importance
to communicate.
But is anybody listening?

Eclipse

Before iron tools, long before bibles,
before the cum-se-wa came,
on that fear-filled noon
when the sun went behind a cloudless sky
and darkness covered the world,
Glesala, supreme among shamen,
wearing his dancing blanket
rattling his rattle
chanting and dancing on the beach
before the village totem poles
did by the power of his magic
bring back the sun from behind the sky
and return light to the world.

There is different magic in the inlet now
and somewhere a different shaman.
His smelter dominates the river flat
where women with their digging sticks sought food.
His ships ride where high-powered canoes once rode.
His town has traffic lights and flashing signs that startle owls.
Its effluent festoons the river's overhanging willows
with shreds of sodden toilet tissue.
His weekend hunters roam ancestral hunting grounds
hunting more for killings than for meat.
In the village, TV aerials surmount
the few remaining totem poles.
The cum-se-wa's totem is Snake-rising-to-strike
from behind two black and upright bars.
It is the universal totem.
Killer Whale, Raven, Thunderbird
lose face before it.

Maggie — in Memory of

In spring when the Skeena runs free of ice,
when swans fly low over the village
and on those crisp Kispiox mornings when the fattening snow
dusts the heads of mountains
Maggie would sometimes stand at her house door
and pray her prayer to the sun.
She inherited the prayer from her grandmother.
This is what it said.
    "O Smaget-ls-ha
    we are your children
    our smoke goes up to you.
    Do not hide your face from us
    or we die."

Maggie gave me permission to use her prayer
when I felt loo-am-cauda, the clean-inside-heart.
She did not tell me I could put the words on paper
but I do not think she would have told me not to.

One winter when good Kitkatla men and women came up river
to set the people's feet on the right path and save their souls
the people went to all the meetings.
Maggie went to only one meeting but no one spoke against her
because of that.
Maggie allowed me to fish at her fishing place.
Its name was Gwinawp. It too had come down to her.
I caught my largest steelhead at Gwinawp.
Maggie had her own small trapline.
She made my moosehide moccasins. Her stitches were strong.
Her smoked salmon were of the best.

October Omen

Slash fire haze distorts the sinking sun.
The sea has been withdrawn.
Exposed rocks have stretched shadows attached to them.
Pilings of the wharf beyond are black
and forbidding as prison bars.

A girl on horseback materializes
from under paper-cut-out firs.
He waves expectantly.
She does not respond.
Horse and rider become two-dimensional
against the darkening afterglow.

Oblivion

Ours is no spirit-broken stream —
From mountain to sea it declares itself.
But when it enters the eternity of Great Waters
its voice is no more heard.

Second Sight

My eyes not being what they were
I make do with bifocals –
and gripe.

Gentle Mary blind from birth
lifts her face to the warming sun –
and smiles.

December Twenty-Fourth

I miss the sleigh bells and the sparkling snow
which marked this season long ago.
But now my heart is gladdened
for beyond the reef I see
a passing ship, and through the rain
its masthead Christmas tree.

The Beholder

She celebrates sunsets and views with pleasure
the distant contours of long-familiar hills.
She sees beauty in the symmetry of drifted snow.

In her eyes the sea before her door
is the majesty of God made manifest.
Her moon is brighter than the moon we see
yet it is the same moon.

She is thankful for each day not knowing
what a day may bring.

She notes the sway of tall grasses in the wind.
Roadside pussywillows in early spring
are tidings of great joy. To her the returning osprey
is confirmation of the covenant.

She sat too long at the feet of her Lady Poverty
and neglected to question the teaching.
Considering the lilies is all very well
But we others have no time to stand and stare.
We have work to do and loads to lift. Moreover
she causes us to question the worth of
things for which we strive.
She is of another time and place.
St. Francis would gladly have shared his crust with her
And Blake his vision of the New Jerusalem.

Star Gazer

The old man lacked schooling and his English was poor
yet he could name and identify constellations
and accurately predict the comings and goings of planets.
He wondered about the universe, pondering its creation
and what lay behind it all. Star gazing was,
in a sense, his religion.

After welfare had him admitted to the nursing home
he somehow managed to get out of bed on clear nights
to stand at windows, contemplating what little sky
could be seen above surrounding buildings.
His clumping along the halls and into and out of rooms
was disturbing and when he persisted
those in charge of the establishment ordered
the sides of his bed raised and locked each night
which, of course, was understandable.

Star gazers of whatever sort
have seldom found favour with establishment
which is why, in various times and places
they have been locked up, put away and
on occasion crucified.

Post Mortem Codicil

(In memory of my friend John Daly. These lines were read at his wake.)

True my calling was the sea and she provided
sustenance for me and mine, but I no longer wish
these few founds of gritty ash – residue of elements
which structured me – to be committed to her keeping
as previously directed.
For in the revealing hour of my departure I knew
that first and last I was a landsman;
scent of balsam on sun-warmed slopes
of juniper at timberline
cloud shadows in pursuit across a mountainside
heather and flowers on alpine meadows
moss tapestries, pastel colourings of wetted stones
these memories and many such remain implanted
in the very substance of my bones.
I therefore direct that my residue be scattered
at valley's head, there to mingle with the residues
of crumbled rock and forest waste until
in earth's good time, the long postponement ended,
all are eroded to the final river
beyond whose splayed and silted mouth
the sea will gather them.

Thoughts while Thinning Carrots

I am thinning carrots
deciding which to save and foster
which to pluck and cast aside.
My decisions are final, there is no appeal.
I am playing god to carrots.

Though not an all-seeing, all-knowing god
My mind wanders and I think of other things
so that, absent-mindedly, I
pluck carrots which should be saved
and save carrots which should be plucked.

Were the circumstances, time and place
of the sparrow's fall decreed
in the Beginning or did they come to pass
by happenstance?
When the cosmic computer was programmed
were the stars fixed eternally in their courses?
Were all worlds that were, are and
evermore shall be, set spinning at
predetermined speeds? Were causes and effects
and effects within causes
(including me here thinning carrots)
irrevocably established, or are they
subject to change without notice?
These and all such questions remain
as my old Scot schoolmaster would say,
"beyond my ken."

What man in his right senses would aspire to be God?

Confidentially

Inept old would-be poet
your huffings and puffings amuse me.
You remind me of that half-drunk glass blower
at our county fair. I paid him ten cents —
all of my weekly allowance — to blow me a swan
but the best he could do was a lopsided bubble.

Viewpoint

When you are ninety
doing that Charlie Chaplin shuffle
down the long road into the sunset
it is not as amusing
as you had thought.

The Gift

Johnny had imagination
make-believe war was his favorite game.
Johnny didn't know the gun was loaded
but they buried his brother just the same.

Imagination was a gift Johnny could have done without
when in combat at twenty his bayonet slew
a fellow in grey who closely resembled
a fellow back home that his kid sister knew.

On parade at the cenotaph year after year
while Last Post bugles soared and yearned
Johnny heard voices, the curses and laughter
of men he had marched with who never returned.

Remembrance Day broadcast last year but one
Johnny tuned in the station then dozed in his chair
his wheezes and snores making ill-timed responses
to a bilingual chaplain's unanswered prayer.

When he roused, the gift was there to haunt him
as with the far vision of unsighted eyes
he saw warheads exploding, the terror and slaughter
mushroom clouds under gun metal skies.

Now for his ease the gift has been returned to sender.
Old wars forgetting, future wars forgot
Johnny rests in peace beside his little brother
six feet under in the family plot.

Questionnaire

What do you make of it all, old man
Now that you're almost there?
The serenity you seek still lies ahead. Press on.
Dismiss the past. Detachment is the order of your day.
What can the inconsequential play of children hold for you?
Why bless young lovers with your following eyes?
Why bare your heart to sorrows other than your own?
Forget your little ship; you will not put to sea again.
The saplings you set out you will never see as trees.
Your compost will nourish gardens someone else will plant.
Why allow your comrade's anguished face to banish sleep?
Why not forget his dismembered body
in that shattered trench?
Why cherish memories of her enduring love?
They will not warm your bed
nor can your arms enfold them.
You pitted will and words against exploiters.
Is it through fault of yours exploiters flourish still?
Had you known the spastic orphan's desolation
before he hanged himself behind the backwoods barn
you would have been the first to offer friendship.
So why accuse yourself that all you did for him
was help to bury him?
You do not answer me, old man
but I know what you are thinking.
For you, detachment is desertion.
For you, and such as you, serenity must wait.

Disadvantaged

Coming from school that afternoon in 1905
Moggie, Bony, Hen and I made up to go frog-swatting
out at the peat beds. We agreed to meet at the top of
the cemetery hill. After reporting home I changed my
blouse and started. My little brother wanted to come
but I told him nix and headed up the street.
At the corner I looked back. Sure enough there he was
tagging after me. I waited and told him skidaddle
on home but he kept following until half way up
the cemetery hill I got so ding-busted mad that
I hauled off and slapped his face.
If he had been anything like our in-between brother
he would have kicked my shins or tried to crown me
with a rock. All this one did was stand there,
his hands at his side, looking up at me with tears
in his eyes. He made me feel like a stinker!
Next thing I knew, I had my arm around him and was
wiping his tears and telling him he could come.

My trouble is I'm too much of a softie.
All my life I've been that way,
always seeing the other person's side of things.
No wonder I never got ahead!

A House Divided

Will there ever be peace in this house of ours?
Always when I retreat to this upper room
seeking to rid my mind of trifles
heed the still small voice
and repossess my soul
I am distracted by their chatter and raffish laughter
in the room below.
Why does he allow such people in?
Allow? He actually welcomes them.
Like as not when I go down
I'll find he's let them turn my cherished pictures
to the wall: the still waters in pastures green
the delectable mountains
Lion and lamb lying down together
and trumpets sounding on the other side.

If only we could part and go our separate ways!
But that's not possible. We are joint tenants
and must remain so as long as the house endures—
and longer still for aught I know.
Oh for some ombudsman, some all-wise arbitrator
to bring peace between us—
between the Me that I mostly am
and the Me that I yearn to be.

Aboriginal Rights

Within easy walking distance of our place
a front-end loader belches, lurches forward
fills its belly with loam and forest seedlings
and regurgitates into a gully.
From the board room of some unconcerned concern ·
the order has gone forth for yet another subdivision.
The developers are upon us. Soon, I fear,
suburbia will displace us.

Faced with expulsion, I remind myself that
my predecessors-thrice-removed were not the first
to set foot on these shoreline acres.
Before they landed with their oxen,
froe, whipsaw, grub-hoes, forge,
two-faced Methodist axes and lesser ictas,
and long before the era of bibles,
copper-toes and sulphur matches,
men of a different race lived, moved and
had their being here. A clamshell midden
at the creekmouth testifies to this.

Nor does the record of displacement end there.
Deep in the great Fraser River midden,
a score of sea miles east of here
skulls were found that are not Salish skulls.
Or so I read.

We all are transients,
dwellers in fly camps along an unblazed trail
leading we know not where.

Other Gods

That long ago day before gillnetting season
Tim and I with our wives and children went up river
in his Haisla poling canoe to picnic together
before we went our separate ways.
We made fire on the bar below the big riffle
and as we sat around it eating, a tiny, high-pitched
somewhat plaintive sound came from the flames.
My son asked what that was and I explained it was merely
steam escaping from the heated wood.
Tim smiled and shook his head. That was Noloch
asking to be fed, he told us. Noloch is the fire spirit
who warms us and cooks our food. We should be grateful to him
and when he asks us, we should feed him.
Still smiling but serious too, Tim took food from his plate
tossed it into the fire and had the children do the same.

Our children live in cities now.
They remember Tim with fondness
and tell his Noloch story to their children.
But how does a child give thanks, make grateful offering to
piped-in gas, or a tank of furnace oil?

In Perpetuity

My shadow will remain on the wall
long after my sun has set.
The winds of change will not efface
my reflection from the secret pool.
The touch of my flesh is remembered by other flesh.
My wanderings beside headlong streams
and in the hanging valleys of desire
are recorded forever.
The echoes of my words repeat themselves.
What was done – is done.
There is no oblivion
Nor easy absolution.